The Bite-sized Bard Presents

Shakespeare's Seasons

CREATED BY
Miriam Weiner

ILLUSTRATIONS BY
Shannon Whitt

EDITED BY MIRIAM WEINER
& SHANNON WHITT

downtown bookworks

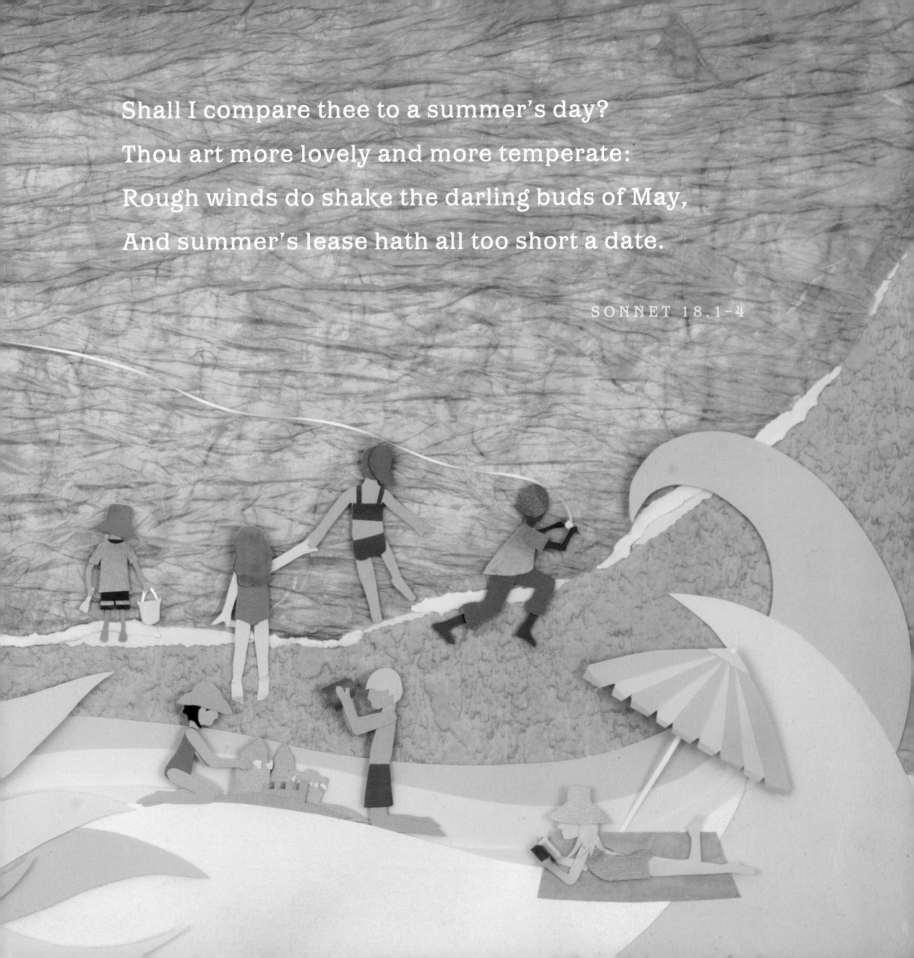

Shall I compare thee to a summer's day?

Thou art more lovely and more temperate:

Rough winds do shake the darling buds of May,

And summer's lease hath all too short a date.

SONNET 18.1–4

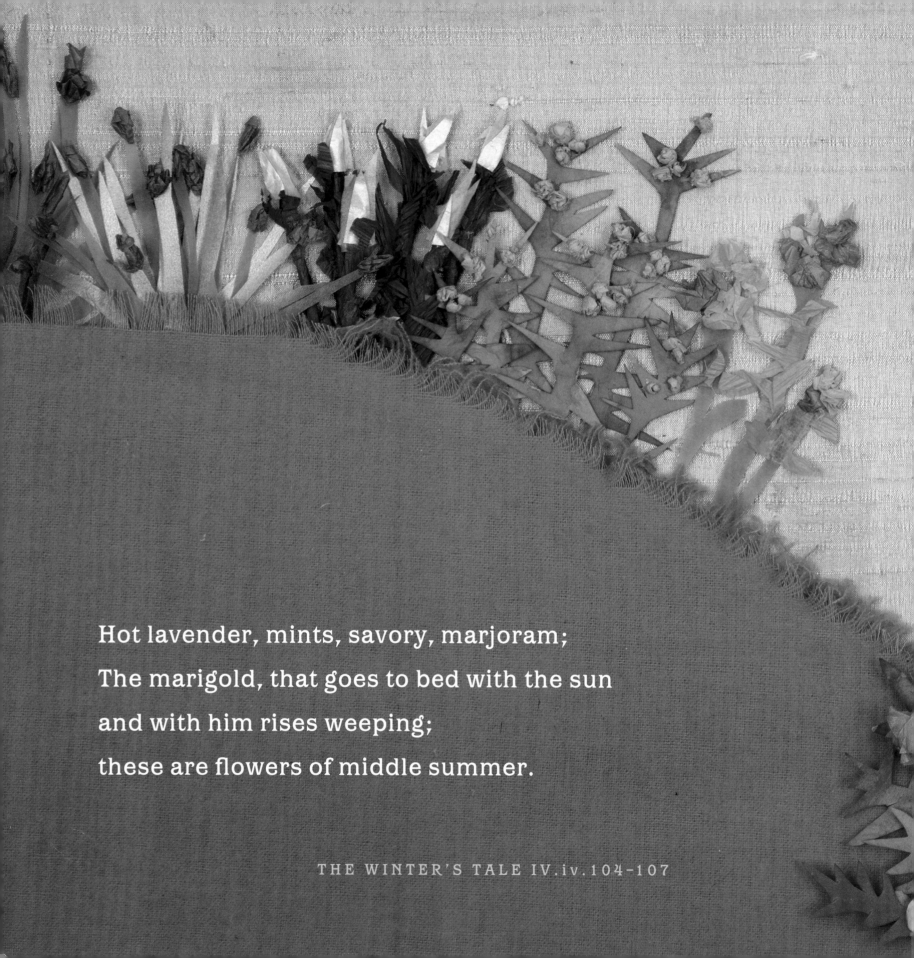

Hot lavender, mints, savory, marjoram;
The marigold, that goes to bed with the sun
and with him rises weeping;
these are flowers of middle summer.

THE WINTER'S TALE IV.iv.104–107

Earth's increase, foison plenty,

Barns and garners never empty,

Vines with clust'ring bunches growing,

Plants with goodly burden bowing;

Spring come to you at the farthest

In the very end of harvest.

Scarcity and want shall shun you,

Ceres' blessing so is on you.

THE TEMPEST IV.i.110-117

For summer and his pleasures wait on thee,

And thou away, the very birds are mute.

Or if they sing, 'tis with so dull a cheer,

That leaves look pale,

dreading the winter's near.

SONNET 97.11-14

and crack your cheeks! Rage! Blow!

KING LEAR III.ii.1

At Christmas

I no more desire a rose

Than wish a snow in May's new-fangled shows,

But like of each thing
that in season grows.

LOVE'S LABOUR'S LOST I.i.105-107

For never resting time leads summer on

To hideous winter and confounds him there;

Sap checked with frost

and lusty leaves quite gone,

Beauty o'ersnowed and

bareness everywhere.

SONNET 5.5-8

But flowers distilled though they with winter meet,

Leese but their show;

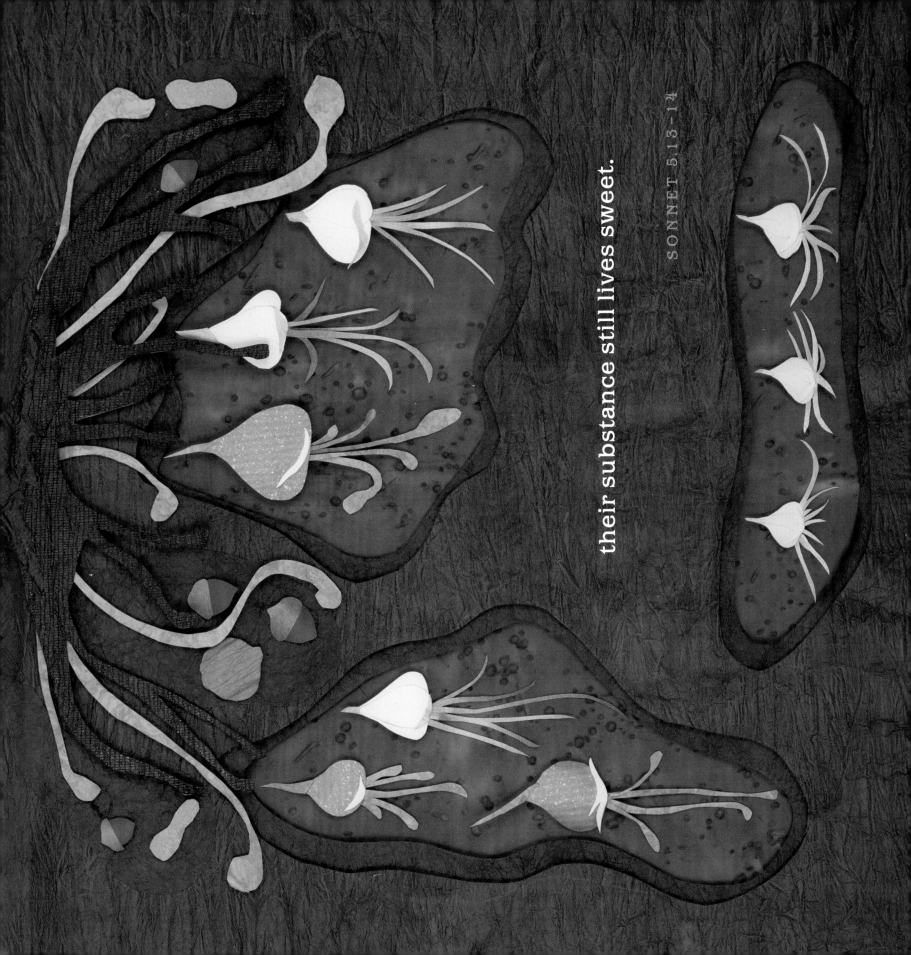

their substance still lives sweet.

SONNET 5.13–14

The purest spring is not so free from mud.

HENRY VI PART 2 III.i.107

The uncertain glory of an April day,

Which now shows all the beauty of the sun,

And by and by a cloud takes all away.

THE TWO GENTLEMEN
OF VERONA I.iii.85–87

This carol they began that hour,

With a hey, and a ho, and a hey nonino,

How that a life was but a flower,

In spring time, the only pretty ring time,

When birds do sing, hey ding a ding, ding,
Sweet lovers love the spring.

AS YOU LIKE IT V.iii.27-32

Blow like sweet roses

in this summer air.

LOVE'S LABOUR'S LOST V.ii.293

Thus sometimes hath
        the brightest day a cloud;

And after summer evermore succeeds
Barren winter,
        with his wrathful nipping cold;

So cares and joys abound,
as seasons fleet.

HENRY VI PART 2 II.iv.1–4

downtown bookworks

Text compilation copyright © 2012 Miriam Weiner

Illustrations copyright © 2012 Shannon Whitt

All rights reserved.

Designed by Georgia Rucker

Art photographed by Ellen Wallop

Printed in China
January 2012

ISBN 978-1-935703-57-0

10 9 8 7 6 5 4 3 2 1

Downtown Bookworks Inc.
285 West Broadway, New York, New York 10013

www.downtownbookworks.com

for: Abel, who inspired; Adam, who arrived; and Gregg who believed.

—Miriam

for Ron, Alberta, Lew, Doris, Becky, Stu
and my dearest Ryan.

—Shannon

Special thanks to Jonathan Lyons.

William Shakespeare is a famous writer
who lived in England about 400 years ago.
During his life, he wrote hundreds of plays,
sonnets, and poems that people still enjoy today.
The way people speak to each other has changed
a bit since Shakespeare's time. This is why some of
the words in this book—words from his sonnets and
plays—may sound funny to you. But listen carefully
and you can enjoy the music of his words, and
the pictures they create in your mind.